The Bill of Rights

by Kirsten Chang

BLASTOFF! READERS

BELLWETHER MEDIA • MINNEAPOLIS, MN

Note to Librarians, Teachers, and Parents:

Blastoff! Readers are carefully developed by literacy experts and combine standards-based content with developmentally appropriate text.

Level 1 provides the most support through repetition of high-frequency words, light text, predictable sentence patterns, and strong visual support.

Level 2 offers early readers a bit more challenge through varied simple sentences, increased text load, and less repetition of high-frequency words.

Level 3 advances early-fluent readers toward fluency through increased text and concept load, less reliance on visuals, longer sentences, and more literary language.

Level 4 builds reading stamina by providing more text per page, increased use of punctuation, greater variation in sentence patterns, and increasingly challenging vocabulary.

Level 5 encourages children to move from "learning to read" to "reading to learn" by providing even more text, varied writing styles, and less familiar topics.

Whichever book is right for your reader, Blastoff! Readers are the perfect books to build confidence and encourage a love of reading that will last a lifetime!

This edition first published in 2019 by Bellwether Media, Inc.

No part of this publication may be reproduced in whole or in part without written permission of the publisher. For information regarding permission, write to Bellwether Media, Inc., Attention: Permissions Department, 6012 Blue Circle Drive, Minnetonka, MN 55343.

Library of Congress Cataloging-in-Publication Data

Names: Chang, Kirsten, 1991- author.
Title: The Bill of Rights / by Kirsten Chang.
Description: Minneapolis, MN : Bellwether Media, Inc., 2019. | Series: Blastoff! Readers: Symbols of American Freedom | Includes bibliographical references and index.
Identifiers: LCCN 2018030413 (print) | LCCN 2018034399 (ebook) | ISBN 9781681036465 (ebook) | ISBN 9781626179158 (hardcover : alk. paper) | ISBN 9781618914927 (pbk. : alk. paper)
Subjects: LCSH: United States. Constitution. 1st-10th Amendments–Juvenile literature. | United States. Constitution. 1st-10th Amendments–History–Juvenile literature. | Civil rights-United States–History–Juvenile literature. | Constitutional amendments–United States–Juvenile literature.
Classification: LCC KF4750 (ebook) | LCC KF4750 .C443 2019 (print) | DDC 342.7303/9–dc23
LC record available at https://lccn.loc.gov/2018030413

Editor: Rebecca Sabelko   Designer: Andrea Schneider

Printed in the United States of America, North Mankato, MN.

Table of **Contents**

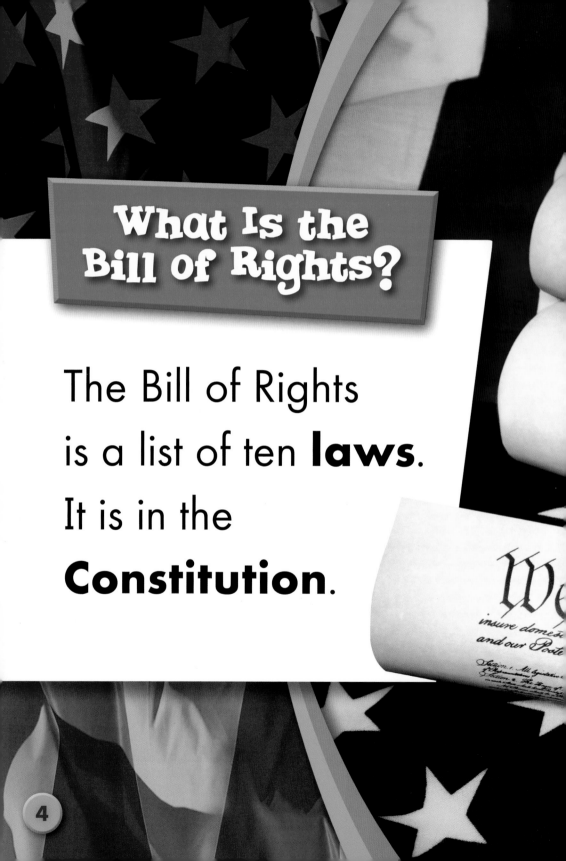

What Is the Bill of Rights?

The Bill of Rights is a list of ten **laws**. It is in the **Constitution**.

IN CONGRESS, JULY 4,

The unanimous Declaration of the thirteen united States

Congress OF THE United

begun and held at the City of New-York, on
Wednesday the Fourth of March, one thousand seven hundred

the People of the United States, in order to form a m
Tranquility provide for the common defence, promote the general Welfare, and secure the
do ordain and establish this Constitution for the United States of America.

Article. I.

5

The laws promise **freedom** to United States **citizens**.

These laws keep the **government** from being too powerful.

History of the Bill of Rights

The Constitution was written in 1787. It states how the government works.

The signing of
the Constitution

But there were no laws for people's **rights**. James Madison wanted to add some.

James
Madison

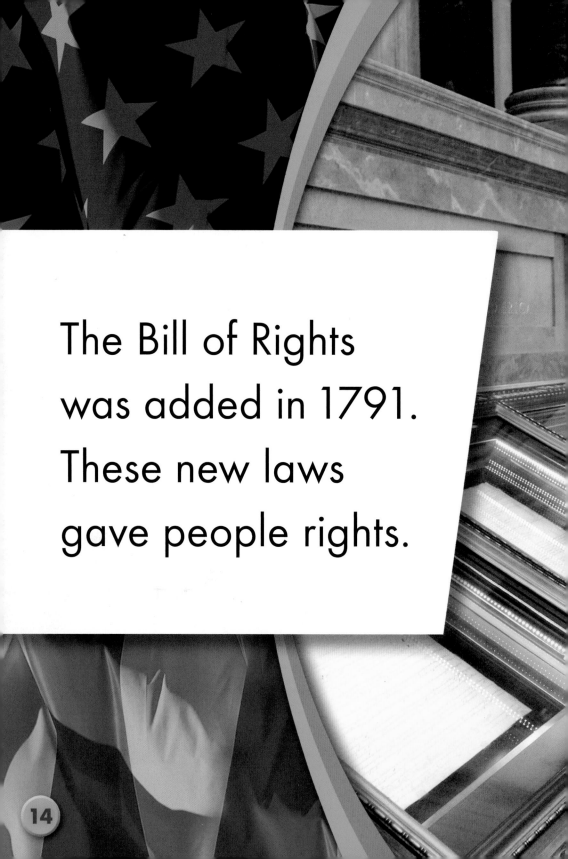

The Bill of Rights was added in 1791. These new laws gave people rights.

people looking at
U.S. Constitution

15

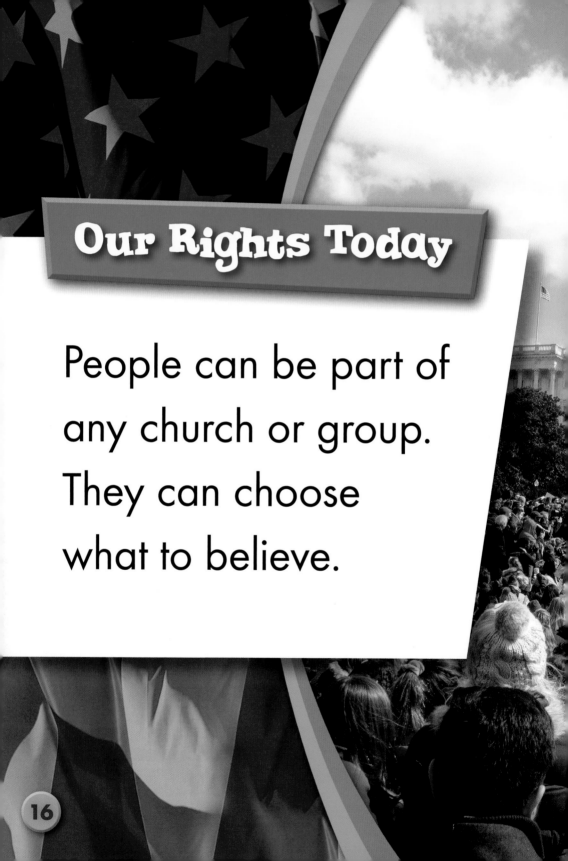

Our Rights Today

People can be part of
any church or group.
They can choose
what to believe.

Our Rights

U.S. citizens have the right to...

 say and believe what they want

 keep themselves safe

 meet in peaceful groups

 be treated fairly by the law

 keep things to themselves

 enjoy other rights given by state governments

People have
the right to be
treated fairly.

WE ARE THE FIRST AMENDMENT

The Bill of Rights
gives us our freedom!

Glossary

citizens

people who live in a certain place

government

the people who make laws and decisions for a city, state, or country

Constitution

the highest law of the U.S. government

laws

rules made by the government that must be followed

freedom

the state of being free

rights

something that a person should be able to have, get, or do

To Learn More

AT THE LIBRARY

McDowell, Pamela. *James Madison*.
New York, N.Y.: AV2 by Weigl, 2014.

Rajczak Nelson, Kristen. *U.S. Constitution*.
New York, N.Y.: PowerKids Press, 2017.

Schuh, Mari. *The United States Constitution*.
Minneapolis, Minn.: Bellwether Media, 2019.

ON THE WEB

FACTSURFER

Factsurfer.com gives you
a safe, fun way to find
more information.

1. Go to www.factsurfer.com.

2. Enter "Bill of Rights" into the search box.

3. Click the "Surf" button and select your
   book cover to see a list of related web sites.

Index